# ANNIE SLOAN

## DECORATIVE
# PAINT EFFECTS

# ANNIE SLOAN

## DECORATIVE
# PAINT EFFECTS

## A PRACTICAL GUIDE

Photography by Geoff Dann

THE READER'S DIGEST ASSOCIATION, INC
Pleasantville, New York/Montreal

A Reader's Digest Book

Conceived, edited, and designed by
Collins & Brown Limited

**Editor** Colin Ziegler
**Editorial Assistant** Claire Waite
**Art Director** Roger Bristow
**Designer** Steve Wooster
**DTP Designer** Claire Graham
**Photographer** Geoff Dann

The acknowledgments that appear on page 96 are hereby made a
part of this copyright page.

Library of Congress Cataloging in Publication Data:

Sloan, Annie, 1949–
        Annie Sloan decorative paint effects : a practical   guide / Annie
Sloan.
        p.  cm.
        Includes index.
        ISBN 0-89577-880-7
        1. House painting.  2. Furniture painting.  3. Texture painting.
I. Title.
TT323.S59   1996
698'. 1–dc20                                              96-2748

Printed in Portugal

# Contents

# Introduction

**T**HE FASCINATING CHARACTERISTIC of the paint techniques shown in this book is that so many effects and variations can be achieved using the same basic materials. The secret ingredient for all the effects is the glaze: a slow-drying, transparent medium that serves as the carrier for the color, whether paint or dry powder pigment. Unlike paint, which dries relatively quickly, glaze dries slowly, allowing you to continue working on

### Ragging

*Ragging (see pp. 22–25) is an adaptable technique that produces an irregular effect. Dab a cotton rag firmly onto wet glaze to reveal the base color in places. The effect is delicate when similar colors are used, and more lively when the contrast between the two – here, terra-cotta on warm yellow – is pronounced.*

### Sponging

*Sponging (see pp. 26–29) is quick and easy to do and produces a regular, dappled effect. You can either sponge on your second color as here – a dark gray has been sponged onto a pale gray basecoat – or you can brush on the second color and then use a sponge to remove it in places.*

### Colorwashing

*Colorwashing (see pp. 30–37) gives a carefree, natural look. By wiping gently over wet glaze with a soft cloth, you remove the brushmarks and give it a loose feel that works particularly well on walls. Choose colors quite close in tone and use the darker one on top – here, warm yellow ocher on off-white.*

a wet surface to produce a decorative finish. Using special brushes, sponges and combs or just everyday materials like rags and newspaper you can create attractive patterns combining base color and glaze color. Since it is transparent, the glaze gives an extra dimension to the paint beneath which remains more or less visible depending on the technique.

Although paint effects may look complicated, they are in fact very easy to do. All the techniques in this book have been carried out with water-base glazes, which are simpler to use than oil glazes especially for the beginner. You can experiment with different mixes: more or less glaze with more or less color to give different degrees of opacity.

### Stippling

*Stippling (see pp. 38–43) provides a very sophisticated, even effect, that, from a distance, can look untextured. It is at its most subtle when a lighter basecoat – here, pale blue – is covered by a darker shade of the same color.*

### Combing

*Combing (see pp. 44–49) creates a strong dramatic finish, since the comb concentrates the top color into lines, allowing the base color to show through clearly. This is most obvious when dark and light colors – here, pale blue on dark red – are used in combination.*

### Dragging and Flogging

*Dragging and flogging (see pp. 50–57) are developed from woodgraining techniques and, by using long, coarse-bristled brushes, produce a variegated, striped look. Flogging (top) gives a more subtle look than dragging (above), but with both the stripes are clearer the greater the color contrast between the basecoat and the glaze.*

Each technique has its own individual character. Some, like stippling (see pp. 38–43) and dragging (see pp. 50–55), lend themselves well to formal situations, particularly when done in traditional colors such as beige or olive green. But in different color combinations, such as terra-cotta over bright yellow with blue dragged horizontally to make a checkered pattern, the look is anything but formal. You get the most dramatic results when you use strongly contrasting colors, while colors close to each other in tone produce a more restrained, conventional look, especially when the glaze color is darker than the color beneath. For greater depth of color you can add a third or even a fourth layer in the same or a different color. And, for added interest, you can

### Patterning with Cloth

*The soft, cloudy look is achieved by using cheese-cloth/mutton cloth, a finely knitted cotton fabric (see pp. 58–61). A piece of the fabric is formed into a small pad and dabbed over the wet glaze. The fabric print leaves a deliberately uneven texture.*

### Rag Rolling

*This effect (see pp. 62–65) uses two techniques: first the glaze is stippled, then, while it is still wet, a crumpled rag is rolled over the surface, removing some of the glaze to reveal the color beneath.*

### Frottage

*Frottage (see pp. 66–71) is a French word meaning "rubbing". This is the only technique that does not use glaze. It is done using thinned-down paint over which an absorbent material such as newspaper or fabric is rubbed. Each new "rubbing" produces a different effect making a random pattern.*

even use different techniques next to each other on the same surface, or even on top of each other.

The most important thing to remember is that you can't go wrong: if you don't like what you have just done, wipe it off and start again. So feel free to experiment and don't worry! Paint effects are great fun to do and very rewarding when you see a room or piece of furniture transformed by your efforts from something commonplace into something unique.

Happy painting!

### Woodgraining

*This is a traditional effect in which paint and glaze are used to imitate wood (see pp. 72–77). Techniques are shown for oak, mahogany, and maple graining – these can be adapted to reproduce other woods. Careful observation and accuracy are needed for successful results.*

### Decorative Graining

*Decorative Graining (see pp. 78–81) is a quick form of woodgraining, using a special tool to make lots of decorative effects, from obviously fake folk woodgraining to producing a finish like moiré or watered silk. Accurate imitation of wood is not the aim.*

### Marbling

*Marbling (see pp. 82–91) is a very old technique and uses a combination of other basic techniques such as sponging and ragging. A badger-hair brush is the essential tool, used to soften the glaze and give it the appearance of smooth marble.*

# Preparing Surfaces

ANY SURFACE THAT CAN BE painted on can be given a special paint effect. The only constraint is that the surface should be a little porous and not too shiny. Glass and ceramics are difficult to paint on but speciality products are available for this purpose. Rough wall surfaces – even brick, stone, unplaned wood, and textured wallpaper – can all be treated, provided an appropriate technique is chosen. However, a smooth surface offers the greatest choice of techniques and the best chance for a successful result. It is worth taking the time, therefore, to fill cracks in walls and strip and sand furniture carefully before painting.

## *Stripping Furniture*

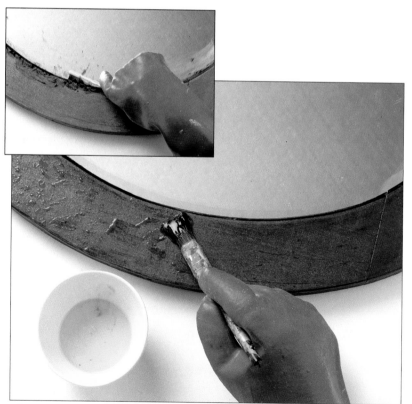

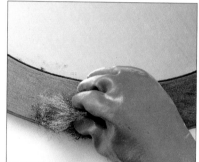

*2 Remove the softened paint or varnish with coarse and then fine steelwool.*

*1 Old paint and varnish must be removed before painting furniture. Wearing rubber gloves, apply chemical stripper over the surface with a paintbrush. Use an old toothbrush to get into the crevices of carved or molded surfaces (inset). Leave the stripper on until the old coat has bubbled up.*

*3 Wipe off excess stripper with an absorbent cloth and the neutralizer recommended by your product. If you are applying water-base varnish, do not use turpentine or white spirit.*

# Filling Cracks

*1* Using a sharp pointed tool such as a screwdriver, dig out the loose plaster from the crack.

*2* Using a trowel, lay a generous amount of filler over the crack. Cover about 18in/45cm at a time.

*3* With the flat edge of the trowel, work the filler into the crack, pulling the trowel down to make a smooth surface.

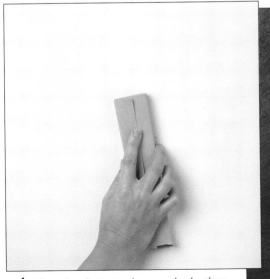

*4* Allow the plaster to dry completely, then rub over the surface with fine-grade sandpaper wrapped around a block of wood (above). Once you have brushed off the dust left by sanding, apply the basecoat in preparation for the glaze (right). If the surface is still not smooth enough, sand it once again and apply another basecoat.

# Basic Equipment

T HE BASIC TOOLS YOU NEED for glazing are the same as for any painting job: drop cloths/dust sheets for protecting floors and furniture, rags for wiping up spills, and rollers and brushes of different sizes for applying the basecoat and glaze. (Speciality brushes are recommended for individual techniques; these are shown on the relevant pages.) For typical painting tasks, the paint you buy is ready-mixed. When glazing, it can be useful to have an assortment of bowls and basins for mixing and experimenting with different colors.

## Applying the Basecoat

*Rollers allow you to apply paint quickly over a large flat area, but they leave a fine "orange peel" texture which you may not want for the final basecoat. For the best results apply the final coat with a brush. Stippling and patterning with cloth, in particular, need a very smooth, even surface. Special brushes are not required, just use one that feels comfortable.*

*Mohair roller*

*Fine sponge roller*

*Smaller brushes for intricate areas and corners*

*Wide flat brushes for covering large areas*

## Applying Glaze

Use flat-ended brushes for applying oil-base glaze and oval-shaped for applying water-base glaze. Several widths of brush may be needed, depending on the size of the surface being covered.

Oval-shaped brushes for applying water-base glaze

Artist's fitch for painting intricate areas

Flat-ended brushes for applying oil-base glaze

## Other Equipment

You will need extra equipment for preparing your glazes and keeping surfaces clean. A plastic bucket or bowl is useful for mixing glazes and glaze colors, and a glass jar is ideal for mixing oil glaze and pigment to the proper consistency. Use a drop cloth or dust sheet to protect the surfaces you do not want paint or glaze to spill on, and a piece of cloth is useful for wiping surfaces clean and removing excess glaze.

Rags for wiping up spills

Plastic paint bucket for mixing glaze

Thin brush for mixing and painting

Bowl for mixing glaze colors

Glass jar

Drop cloth/dust sheet

# Types of Glaze

**M**OST PAINT EFFECTS are achieved with a glaze, which is a translucent medium that can be colored with paint or pigment. Colored glaze is applied to the surface and then manipulated into patterns with cloths, brushes, and sponges, revealing in places the color of the basecoat underneath. Both water- and oil-base glazes are now available. Oil-base glazes (see opposite) were used traditionally and are still preferred by some professional painters and decorators since they can give greater depth of color. However, they are now being superseded by water-base glazes, which are easy to use and more environmentally friendly. In this book we use water-base glazes, although the technique is similar whichever glaze you use.

## Normal Water-base Glaze

*Use this type of glaze for all the decorative paint techniques in this book except for woodgraining and marbling (see below). To color it simply add water-base paint. On a satin-finish basecoat it will produce a crisp look and on a flat basecoat the effect will be dry and chalky. It is easier to use it over a middle-sheen finish since the glaze will quickly soak into a flat basecoat, giving you less time to work.*

## Water-base Glaze for Use with Universal Stainers and Pigments

*Use this type of glaze for woodgraining and marbling since it creates a very transparent look that both techniques require. Color the glaze by adding universal stainers or pigment – add a little at a time, until you have the required degree of opacity. This type of glaze dries quite quickly so apply it to small areas at a time.*

*Water-base paint*

*Normal water-base glaze*

*Water-base glaze for woodgraining and marbling*

*Dry powder pigment*

*Universal stainers or colorizers*

## Store-bought Oil-base Glazes

Oil-base glaze can be bought either in a transparent form or as "scumble" glaze which is pre-colored in wood colors. It is made with plant-based substances such as linseed oil and turpentine. To use the clear glaze you mix one part oil-base glaze with one part turpentine, and then color with pigments or oil-base paint. You should use them over a middle-sheen or eggshell basecoat.

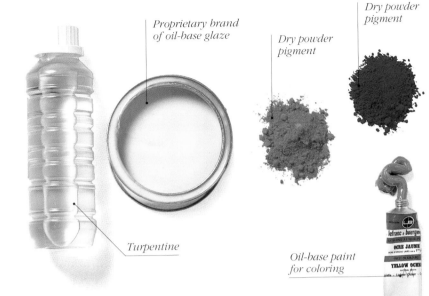

*Proprietary brand of oil-base glaze*

*Dry powder pigment*

*Dry powder pigment*

*Turpentine*

*Oil-base paint for coloring*

## Homemade Oil-base Glazes

Everyone has their own recipe but you basically mix "boiled linseed oil", turpentine, and a dryer (to accelerate the drying time) in roughly equal proportions and then color with pigment or oil paint. They are usually used over oil-base paints, but some water-base paints are also suitable.

*Dry powder pigment*

*Oil-base paint*

*Dryer*

*Turpentine*

*Boiled linseed oil*

# Using Glazes

THE AMOUNT OF PAINT or coloring agent that you mix in with your glaze depends on how opaque you want your glaze to be. The more paint you add the more opaque the effect will be. With normal water-base glaze (see p. 14) you should mix four to six parts glaze to one part paint. Remember that the more paint there is, the quicker it dries, leaving less time to complete your effect.

Your prime concern is that the glaze does not dry out before you complete your effect. If glazing a large area therefore, apply the glaze in sections for certain techniques and in strips for others.

**Levels of Opacity**
*Glaze can have either a lot or a little paint mixed with it. The more paint is added the more opaque the effect. Here, a green glaze was applied over a blue ragged background. On the left it was simply painted on, while on the right it was also ragged. The progression from top to bottom shows that when more and more paint is added, the background blue is obliterated.*

# Painting in Sections

*1* For ragging, sponging, stippling, colorwashing, patterning with cloth, and some combing techniques, apply the glaze over an area about 18 in/45 cm square.

*2* Carry out the required technique on the glaze, leave an unworked strip on one side, known as the wet edge. Paint the next area of glaze right into this so that a line is not created where the two sections meet.

# Painting in Strips

*1* For dragging, flogging, and some combing techniques, apply the glaze in a strip from ceiling to molding. Drag, flog, or comb down, leaving a wet edge so the next strip can be joined invisibly. Wipe off any glaze that has spread onto the molding.

*2* Drag or flog from the bottom of the wall by drawing the brush upward. This helps to break up the brushmarks and to avoid a build-up of glaze at the edge.

## GLAZING ON RAISED SURFACES

Paint effects also work well on rough or irregular surfaces such as raised wallpaper. You can either choose a technique to mask the texture or to accentuate it. As a general rule choose an effect that produces an irregular, highly patterned surface, such as ragging, to disguise a pattern and a plain, smooth effect, such as colorwashing, to enhance it. However this does depend on the pattern you are glazing over. You can see how the pattern on the wallpaper below is far more noticeable after it has been dragged as opposed to stippled, since the basecoat shows through, emphasizing the pattern on the dragging.

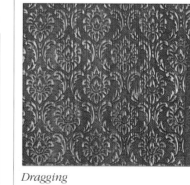

*Dragging*

*Stippling*

# Varnishes and Waxes

THERE ARE TWO REASONS FOR varnishing or waxing over a paint effect: for protection and for decorative effect. Glazed paint effects are relatively durable, but they need a protective coating if used on an object or area that gets hard wear. Wax does offer some protection but varnish is best for areas that need to be wiped over frequently, such as tabletops, kitchen, or bathroom cupboards or walls, that may get marked or scraped. Dark colors often look good with gloss varnish, while mellow, earthy colors are better enhanced by wax or matt varnish.

## Satin (semigloss) Varnish

*Both the paint sample and molding are covered with a coat of water-base, also known as acrylic, varnish. The varnish is quick-drying and has a glossy finish. You could create the same effect with an oil-base glossy varnish. The latter takes longer to dry but gives the surface a slight yellow tinge that emphasises and deepens the colors.*

*Varnish brush*

*Satin water-base varnish*

## Flat Varnish

*Water-base flat varnish protects the surface without making it greaseproof. For stronger protection with a flat finish first coat your surface with a satin varnish, and then with a flat varnish. Completely flat oil-base varnishes are difficult to obtain. Here, the paint sample and molding were coated with a flat water-base varnish tinted with a green pigment. Pigment can be added to all varnishes or you can buy colored varnishes ready-made.*

*Varnish brush*

*Colored flat water-base varnish*

## APPLYING VARNISH AND WAX

You should apply varnish in a thin, even layer using a flat brush. Brush it out with the tip of the brush.

Apply wax with very soft, fine-grade steelwool. Leave it for 10 to 15 minutes so the wax penetrates the surface and then buff it with a soft cloth.

*Applying varnish*

*Applying wax*

## Clear Wax

*This offers some protection to the surface, but not as much as varnish. It imparts a soft, attractive sheen far from the deadening finish of flat varnish but less shiny than gloss or satin varnish. You must use a wax which does not contain Toluene since this is a paint stripper.*

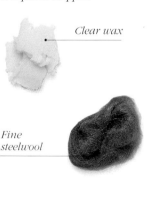

*Clear wax*

*Fine steelwool*

*Cotton cloth*

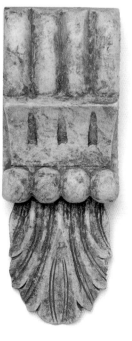

## Dark Wax

*You can use a dark-colored wax to create an aged or antiqued look. Here, dark-colored wax was used to darken the colors on both the paint sample and the molding. On the latter it was allowed to settle more thickly in the crevices, simulating grime accumulated over the years.*

*Dark wax*

*Soft steelwool*

*Cotton cloth*

# Techniques

Ragging

Sponging

Colorwashing

Stippling

Combing

Dragging & Flogging

Patterning with Cloth

Rag Rolling

Frottage

Woodgraining

Decorative Graining

Marbling

Combining Techniques

# Ragging

**Ragged Wall**

*A yellow ocher glaze, darkened with a hint of terra-cotta red, was ragged over an off-white background. When choosing the color combinations for your wall, avoid highly contrasting colors unless you want a very dramatic effect.*

RAGGING PRODUCES a lively irregular pattern that is suitable for decorating both walls and pieces of furniture. You bunch a rag the size of a large napkin in your hand and then dab it firmly onto the wet glaze, so that it removes the glaze in parts, revealing the base color underneath. A soft cotton rag is most commonly used, but different materials make different patterns depending on their thickness and absorbency – heavy linen, for instance, makes a bold crisp effect, while polyester cloth gives a lighter, more undefined look.

The color of the basecoat is vital in ragging because so much of it is revealed. The standard style is to cover it with a glaze a few tones darker – the more similar the colors are, the subtler the effect.

## TOOLS & MATERIALS

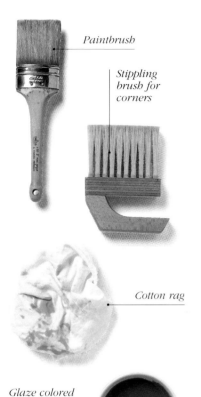

*Paintbrush*

*Stippling brush for corners*

*Cotton rag*

*Glaze colored with water-base paints*

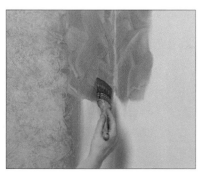

# The Basic Technique

*1* Apply a liberal coat of glaze over a maximum area of 20 in/130 cm square, using criss-cross brushstrokes.

*2* Dab a bunched-up rag over the wet glaze to lift it off. Leave a strip unragged along the edges.

*3* After about 10 dabs, re-form the rag so it doesn't become saturated. When the whole rag is sodden, replace it with a new one.

*4* Repeat Steps 1 and 2 until you have covered the whole surface.

# Avoiding Glaze Build-up in Corners

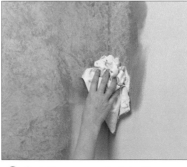

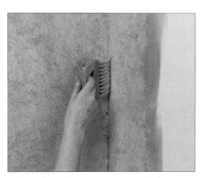

*1* Apply glaze to the surface in the same way as in The Basic Technique, *but be careful so it's not too thick in the corner.*

*2* Dab the rag gently into the corner, applying more pressure to one side than the other to prevent the glaze from being smeared.

*3* When the glaze is nearly dry – after about half an hour – dab firmly into the corner with a stippling brush to remove any excess glaze.

# Special Effects

*It is usual to rag until the brushmarks are no longer visible. But you can make a special feature of them by leaving parts of the surface unragged.*

*Over small areas, such as panels, you can make a pattern by dabbing at regular intervals while keeping the rag in the same position in your hand.*

# Double Ragging

*When the glaze is dry, you layer in a different color, or a deeper shade of the same color, to intensify the effect. This also lets you adjust a color that is not quite right.*

## PITFALLS

A layer of glaze that is too thick results in a glutinous and bubbly surface (below). A layer of glaze that is spread too far or made with only a little paint will make a weak effect when ragged (bottom).

*Glaze too thick*

*Glaze too thin*

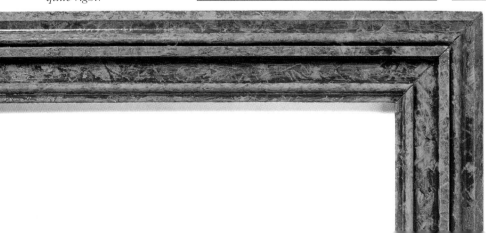

## Ragged Frame

*LEFT This frame was covered with a coat of cool gray-blue and then ragged over with a warm chocolate-brown glaze.*

## Double-Ragged Box

*BELOW The yellow ocher basecoat on this box was ragged over twice in a dark red to give a greater intensity of color.*

## Ragged Candlestick

*LEFT The dark, subtle effect on this candlestick was achieved by ragging a rich, clear blue over a brown basecoat.*

## COLOR COMBINATIONS

*Dark red on light gray*

*Dark green on paler green*

*Yellow ocher on terra-cotta red*

*Dark blue on off-white*

## RAGGING WITH OTHER MATERIALS

Plastic wrap and other types of plastic give a strong, clearly defined pattern that works well on furniture. If you use it on walls, keep the colors close in tone to stop the effect from being overwhelming. Paper towel works well on all surfaces. It gives a soft, slightly spotted finish.

*Plastic wrap*

*Paper towel*

*Using plastic wrap*

*Using paper towel*

# Sponging

**Sponged Tabletop**

*The deep, rich color of this tabletop was achieved by sponging several shades of turquoise together with a little brighter green for contrast over a black basecoat. Layers were built up for a dense effect.*

S PONGING PRODUCES a lively, informal effect that can be achieved in two different ways. Both are quick and easy to do. You can apply colored glaze with a brush over the basecoat – which can be either darker or lighter in tone – and then partially remove it with a sponge. This is called "sponging off". Or, the glaze can be applied directly with a sponge, called "sponging on". A natural sea sponge gives good results by making small, irregular spots of color. Sponging off creates a denser effect, while sponging on gives a lighter look. Responging with other colors gives greater depth. Sponging on can be done just using paint without mixing in a glaze, especially on small areas, but the use of glaze helps to build up translucent layers of color, adding to the impression of depth.

## TOOLS & MATERIALS

*Brush for
applying glaze*

*Large
sponge*

*Small sponge
for sponging
in corners*

*Blue glaze*

# The Basic Technique

**1** *Generously paint on the colored
glaze. The brushstrokes can be
uneven, but the background surface
should be well covered.*

**2** *With a damp sponge, dab all
over the glaze, pressing firmly to
disguise any brushstrokes. Change the
angle of your wrist to avoid a regular
pattern. Leave a wet edge.*

**3** *Again using a brush,
work into the wet edge,
applying a generous
amount of glaze for the
next section.*

**4** *Continue as before, sponging over the
brushstrokes. Rinse the sponge in a bucket
of water when it has absorbed a lot of glaze,
squeezing out well.*

# Sponging a Corner

**1** *Brush the glaze on
both walls and into the
corner, working it well in.
Dab off the glaze from the
walls as explained in
The Basic Technique.*

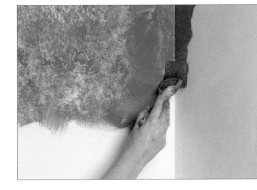

**2** *In order to dab right into the
corner, use a small sponge or
break off a piece of the large sponge.*

# Double Sponging

You can achieve interesting effects by building up layers of different colors. Dab on colors next to each other or overlap them to produce a third color. Sponging on and sponging off can also be mixed. Sponging off often gives a more solid base, over which you can sponge on other colors or tones to create depth and highlights. Or, sponge on several colors to give a subtly flecked effect.

**1** *Use two, three, four, or more colors to build up density. Here, the first color is applied lightly, letting the background show through.*

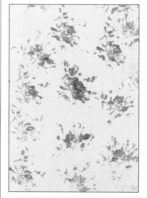

**2** *The second and third layers of glaze, in dark red and pale yellow, are applied. The previous layer may be slightly wet, but if you make a mistake you will have to start again.*

**3** *The final layer, dark blue-gray glaze, is applied. Painting on a layer of varnish between layers protects previous work if you have to wipe off or reapply glaze.*

# Using Synthetic Sponges

*Using rectangular synthetic sponges gives a very different result from natural sponges. Here, a deliberately hard-edged effect is created using different sized sponges with two colors of glaze.*

## PITFALLS

Sponging on is less successful if the glaze color contrasts too much with the color of the basecoat (below left). Also, if the sponging is too far apart – leaving large gaps – the effect is patchy. Sponging off looks heavy and coarse if the glaze is too thick and dark (below right).

*Too much contrast and too far apart*

*Glaze too thick*

## Sponged Wall

*ABOVE A pink-toned terra-cotta glaze was applied with a brush over an off-white basecoat. The glaze was then sponged off to produce an evenly dappled effect.*

## Sponged Candlestick

*RIGHT The stone effect on this candlestick was achieved by sponging on shades of ocher, gray, and dark cream irregularly over a cream base.*

## COLOR COMBINATIONS

*Dark green, then khaki, on pale olive green*

*Black on bright blue*

*Yellow ocher on deep red*

*Deep red on bright green*

## Striped Wall

*ABOVE Blue and white stripes were painted on the wall with a roller. Pale blue was sponged over the blue and a darker blue over the white.*

## Sponged Chair

*ABOVE The chair was first painted blue then reds and yellows were sponged on the seat and back slats.*

# Colorwashing

THIS TECHNIQUE RESULTS in different characteristics depending on the colors you use. With earthy ochers the effect is reminiscent of an old lime-washed wall with contrasting dark and faded patches. With strong, rich colors, such as crimson or emerald green, the result is like oriental lacquer, especially when enhanced with a coat of gloss or satin varnish. Soft pastel colors look best either left natural or with a coat of flat varnish (see pp. 18–19). Unlike other paint techniques, which are carried out in strips or patches, you can cover a large surface area with glaze at a time because, when colorwashing, you only wipe or brush off the glaze when it is nearly dry to avoid leaving scratch marks. If the glaze dries out too much you can use a lightly dampened cloth.

## Colorwashed Fireplace

*The simple shape of this fireplace was given interest by subtle colorwashing. Over a basecoat of pale blue-gray, glazes of blue, mahogany red, and a dark mixture of the two were applied in patches of varying intensity. The glazes were lightly wiped over, allowed to dry, then reapplied to strengthen the depth of color. The sides of the mantel shelf and edges of the side panels were wiped off with a soft cloth while the glaze was still wet to create a contrasting border.*

This detail shows the contrast between the colorwashed effect built up in several layers and the paler edges where the top layers of glaze have been wiped off.

## TOOLS & MATERIALS

*Paintbrush for applying glaze*

*Smaller brush for corners and edges*

*Cheesecloth/ mutton cloth*

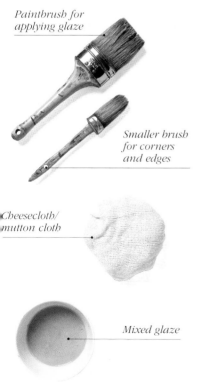

*Mixed glaze*

# The Basic Technique

**1** *Paint the glaze over the whole area to be covered and allow it to dry until it can be worked on without scratching the glaze. If the area is too large the glaze may dry too quickly, in which case work in patches, leaving a wet edge to work into.*

**2** *Wipe over the wall with a soft cloth, using strokes of different lengths in all directions. Press hard enough to expose the basecoat but not to remove all the glaze.*

**3** *The cloth will become saturated with glaze as you work, so refold it and begin wiping again with a fresh section of cloth.*

**4** *Continue smoothing out the glaze with the cloth until all the brushmarks are hidden and the color is evenly spread.*

# Colorwashing Above a Dado Rail

*1* Using a 3 in/75 mm paintbrush, apply a generous
layer of glaze to the area of the wall above the
dado rail, taking care not to come too close to the
dado rail itself.

*2* Using a smaller brush (here, 1½ in/38 mm), apply the
glaze carefully right up to the edge of the rail. Do not
overload the brush.

*4* Using a small cloth pad, wipe off
any excess glaze in the recess
between rail and wall.

*3* When the glaze is almost dry, wipe it off in all
directions using a soft cloth (see The Basic
Technique, p. 31, steps 2–4).

# Double Colorwashing

A second layer of glaze in a different color, or in a different shade of the first color, can be applied to intensify, deepen or lighten the first layer. The bigger the contrast between the two colors you choose, the more distinct the effect, since when the second glaze layer is wiped off, the background color will show through. To alter the look further, you can then apply more layers if desired.

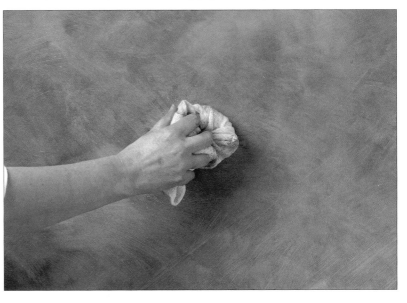

*1 Brush on the second layer of glaze (here, reddish brown) when the first layer (here, pale yellow ocher) is dry (see* The Basic Technique, *p. 31).*

*2 When the surface is nearly dry, wipe over it with a soft rag ,removing some of the second layer and allowing the first color to show through.*

# Colorwashing a Cornice

*1 This technique suits any carved or molded surface. Using a color a few tones darker than the basecoat, paint the glaze on with a small brush, working it well into the crevices.*

*2 When the glaze is nearly dry, wipe gently over the molded surface with a soft cloth. You may need to apply more pressure in certain areas to get an even look.*

# Colorwashing a Carved Object

Colorwashing can be used to emphasize the depth of carving and molding. The darker colored glaze or paint accumulates in the crevices but is wiped off the raised areas, which, being lighter, then appear more prominent. This technique gives a pleasantly "aged" look to a new object such as the plaque shown here, as the darker color resembles dirt that has built up in the crevices over the years.

*1* *For a denser effect use paint rather than glaze. Having painted on the basecoat (here, deep terra-cotta) and varnished it (see pp. 18–19) to prevent the second coat from being absorbed by the plaster of the plaque, paint on the second coat (here, brown-black).*

*2* *When the paint is nearly dry, gently wipe a soft cloth over the face, using more pressure on the raised surfaces to remove more of the darker paint and so highlight the molding.*

*3* *If the paint has dried or more needs to be removed, wipe over the raised areas with a lightly dampened cloth.*

### The Finished Plaque
RIGHT *The contrast between the lighter and darker areas on the finished plaque gives a convincing antique effect.*

# Using More than Two Colors

*1* *You can apply more than two colors side by side, rather than overlaying them as in double colorwashing. First paint on patches of glaze (here, green), leaving spaces for the next color.*

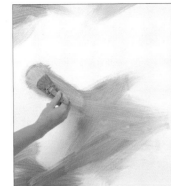

*2* *Cover all the empty areas with another layer of glaze in a color of similar intensity (here, light blue). To give strength and contrast, also dab on small patches of paint in a third color (here, dark blue).*

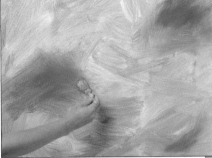

*3* *Brush out the paint thoroughly to merge the darker color into the glaze. The colors should flow into each other, without any harsh edges.*

*4* *Wipe all over the surface with a soft cloth in a circular polishing motion, smoothing out the colors. The result should be a soft, cloudy effect.*

## COLORWASHING WITH BRUSHES

You can use brushes instead of a cloth to wipe off the glaze; this gives a coarser effect, showing the marks of the bristles. For a softer look, hold the tip of the brush at right angles to the surface and wipe gently as with a cloth. A soft wallpaper brush leaves less distinct lines than a hard brush.

*Wallpapering brush*

*House painter's brush*

*Colorwashing with a hard brush*

*Colorwashing with a soft brush*

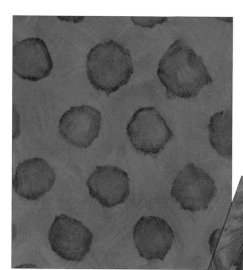

## Blue over Green

*ABOVE The peppermint green basecoat was colorwashed with sage green glaze. When dry, spots of blue glaze were dabbed on and the center of each was immediately wiped off lightly.*

## Colorwashed Door

*RIGHT The bright orange basecoat on the door frame was colorwashed with rich brown glaze. On the panels, the green basecoat was covered with deep blue glaze, which was wiped off in places to make tree shapes and other patterns.*

## Terra-cotta over Orange

*ABOVE A terra-cotta glaze was brushed over an orange basecoat. This was wiped off by twisting a cloth to create swirls.*

## Rustic Letter Rack

*LEFT This look was created by colorwashing a clear middle-blue glaze over a bright yellow basecoat.*

## PITFALLS

Colorwashing is usually done by wiping off the glaze in all directions. If you wipe it off in one direction – here, diagonally, (near right) – it looks less even. To achieve depth of color, it is better to apply two thin layers of glaze. If you apply one thick one the effect looks too heavy (far right).

*Wiping off in one direction*

*Glaze too thick*

## Classical Plaque

*RIGHT The plaque was covered with a coat of light gray-brown paint; then a dark glaze made from several shades of brown was painted over it. The surface was wiped over lightly to remove the glaze from the raised areas.*

## COLOR COMBINATIONS

*Dark blue-green on bright green*

*Brown/mauve on beige*

*Yellow ocher on warm cream*

*Middle-blue on pale blue*

## Colorwashing with a Dado Rail

*LEFT The muddy pink basecoat on this wall was colorwashed with dark crimson red glaze above the rail. Below it, the same glaze was used, with a little chocolate brown added.*

## Colorwashing with a Cornice

*LEFT The wall beneath the white cornice has been colorwashed very simply with one layer of raw sienna over an off-white basecoat.*

# Stippling

**Stippled Plaque and Wall**

*Both the wall and the plaque have been stippled with a green glaze so that they harmonize with each other even though the base colors are completely different. The wall was painted bright lemon yellow while the basecoat on the plaque is gray.*

THIS CLASSIC TECHNIQUE gives a delicate, sophisticated effect. A thin, almost translucent layer of glaze is applied over the basecoat and hit with a special brush while still wet. The brush breaks up the glaze into small spots – though these can only be seen from close up – allowing the base color to show through. When choosing your colors, make sure that the glaze contains a high concentration of color since it needs to be spread very thinly. Use a white basecoat to show off primary colors, but for more muted shades, off-white may be more suitable. Colored bases will give richer, more complex finishes. Whatever colors you use, stippling works best on very smooth surfaces since it shows up every bump and imperfection.

## TOOLS & MATERIALS

*Mixed glaze and brush*

*3 x 4in/75 x 100mm stippling brush for small areas*

*1 x 4in/25 x 100mm stippling brush for corners and details*

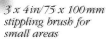

*5 x 7in/127 x 178mm stippling brush for larger surfaces*

# The Basic Technique

*1* Cover the surface with a layer of glaze, brushing it in all directions to spread it out very thinly.

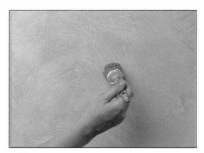

*2* Go over the surface gently with the tip of the brush to make it as smooth and even as possible and to remove any brushmarks.

*3* Using a large stippling brush, hit the surface with a steady, strong motion. Move on to the next area, repeating the action and overlapping the previous area each time. The finished effect should be evenly and finely speckled.

# Dealing with Specks

*2* Wipe the stippling brush regularly with a cloth to remove the glaze that will accumulate on the bristles. Excess glaze on the brush will spoil the even effect you are aiming for.

*1* Small blobs or specks of glaze are sometimes left from stippling. Remove these with your finger and stipple again immediately.

# Stippling a Corner

*1* *Stipple up to the corner then using a small brush, paint the glaze right into the corner.*

*2* *Stipple one wall as far into the corner as possible without hitting the other wall.*

*3* *Stipple the other wall in the same way. Keep the bristles of the brush parallel to the surface of the wall and wipe off excess glaze from the brush as you work.*

*4* *Using the smallest size stippling brush – 1 x 4in/25 x 100mm – stipple right into the corner, wiping off excess glaze. If you find that too much glaze is being removed, allow the glaze to dry a little before continuing.*

# Stippling from Light to Dark

*1* *First apply a band of the lightest colored glaze over the surface, spreading it out thinly and evenly (see* The Basic Technique, *p. 39, Steps 1–2).*

*2* *Leaving a gap below the first band – here 2–3in/ 5–7.5cm – apply another band of the same color in the same way as in Step 1.*

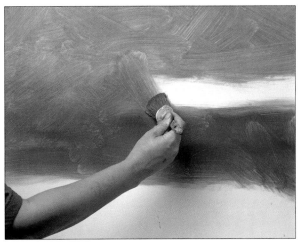

*3* While the second (lower) band is still wet, cover it with a second coat of glaze in the darker colored glaze, spreading it out evenly and thinly.

*4* Brush the glaze out over the gap to join the darker color to the lighter color above it. Brush well over the edges so that the shades merge. Repeat Steps 2–4 using two layers of the darker colored glaze.

*5* Stipple the whole area as directed in The Basic Technique (see p. 39), starting at the top in the lightest area and working downward into the darkest area. Working in this direction ensures that you do not take more glaze back into the paler area. When you have finished (right) the different colored bands should be barely perceptible, with the color just gradually becoming darker towards the bottom.

# Stippling a Dado Rail

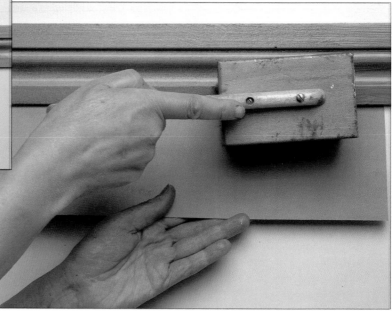

**1** Paint the glaze over the rail, taking care to spread it out evenly and not allow too much glaze to accumulate in the crevices.

**2** Using a smaller stippling brush – here 3 x 4in/75 x 100mm – stipple evenly along the surface, changing the angle at which you direct the brush to avoid brushmarks. Hold a piece of cardboard against the edge of the rail to protect the wall above and below.

## PITFALLS

If you hit the stippling brush too hard on the surface you will create small lines and stripes (near right). Although this is not the classic effect, it could be used as a deliberate technique in itself. If the stippling brush is not hit hard enough against the surface (far right), the brush-marks of the original glaze application will be visible and you will not achieve a satisfactory stippled effect.

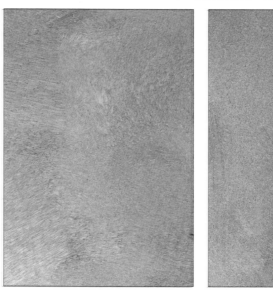

*Hitting too hard*

*Hitting too lightly*

## Lamp Base

*LEFT This white lamp base was stippled with blue glaze mixed with a little white to lighten it. To get an even finish, you need to stipple the surface delicately and steadily while gradually rotating the lamp base.*

# COLOR COMBINATIONS

Blue on pink

Middle-blue on pale lemon

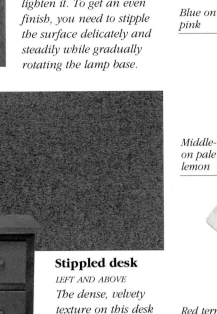

## Stippled desk

*LEFT AND ABOVE*
*The dense, velvety texture on this desk was achieved by stippling a cool shade of brown over the warm yellow ocher basecoat. This calm combination suggests natural wood grain.*

Red terra-cotta on orange

## STIPPLING WITH OTHER BRUSHES

Any brush with short, rigid bristles can be used for stippling with less perfect, but still interesting results. The clusters of bristles in a dustpan brush, for example, leave a noticeable pattern (right).

*Clothes brush*

*Dustpan brush*

*Stippling with a dustpan brush*

Dark green on middle-green

# Combing

COMBS WERE ORIGINALLY USED for some types of woodgraining, but today are used for many other decorative effects, such as making stripes, checks, and borders. Traditional and contemporary sources can both provide inspiration: tartans, ginghams, madras plaids, and Regency stripes can all suggest stunning color combinations. When combing, the colors you use are more crucial than in other paint effects, which rely on the translucency of the glaze to enhance and deepen the base color. The glaze should be almost completely opaque when combing so that the lines that are created are clear and strong.

**Tartan Table**

*The table was first painted red. When the paint was dry, broad stripes of green glaze were painted across the width of the table and combed with a graduated comb (see* Tools and Materials*). When this coat dried, rich blue stripes were painted on in the opposite direction and combed in the same way. Regularly spaced fine lines in pale yellow were painted on to complete the tartan effect.*

## TOOLS & MATERIALS

*Triangular comb with three different widths of teeth*

*Graduated comb with two widths of teeth*

*Glaze*

*Glazing brush*

*Rag for wiping glaze off combs*

# The Basic Technique

*1* Paint glaze over the area to be combed, making it as even as possible. If combing a wall, cover an area approximately 3 feet (1 meter) wide, from ceiling to floor.

*2* Holding the comb in both hands, with the teeth slanted upward, pull it down carefully from the top. Do it quite quickly to avoid wobbles.

*3* If you need to stop halfway, avoid making horizontal lines by lightly relaxing the pressure on the surface before removing the comb.

# Double Combing

Homemade (see p. 46) and store-bought combs offer teeth with varying widths, both regular and graduated. The possibilities they provide when used in double, triple, or even more layers produce an unlimited variety of combed stripes and checks. Try light, bright colors over dark colors, and vice versa. Below, a graduated comb is used twice to make a checkered pattern.

*1* Once the previously combed surface has dried completely, cover it with a different colored glaze, spreading it out as evenly as possible.

*2* Comb across horizontally. Position yourself for maximum stabilty and hold the comb in both hands.

# Making a Comb

While it is possible to buy long-lasting, strong but supple combs, these may not be exactly the right size for your project. You can easily make your own combs using strong cardboard, but they will not last long, since the paper softens and absorbs paint. Soft plastic floor tiles are excellent for homemade combs since they are easy to cut but durable.

*1　Cut a rectangular shape in a flexible plastic floor tile. Mark the edge at regular intervals according to the width of tooth and spacing you want.*

*2　Draw a pencil line parallel to the edge and then draw "V" shapes between every second mark with the base of the "V" facing inward.*

*3　Carefully cut out the "V" shapes with a sharp knife, leaving blunted teeth.*

*4　Trim off the edges of the comb diagonally to make it easier to handle.*

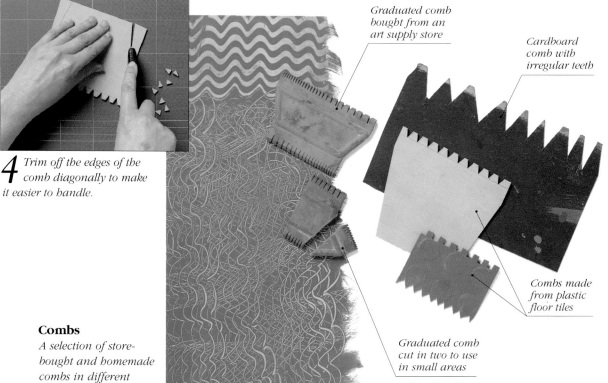

**Combs**
*A selection of store-bought and homemade combs in different materials and sizes.*

*Graduated comb bought from an art supply store*

*Cardboard comb with irregular teeth*

*Combs made from plastic floor tiles*

*Graduated comb cut in two to use in small areas*

# Checkerboard Combing

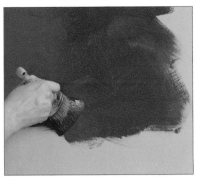

*1* *Apply the glaze with a brush, spreading it out well. The glaze should contain enough paint to make it opaque.*

*2* *Using a comb with broad, regularly spaced teeth, make alternate vertically and horizontally combed squares (right).*

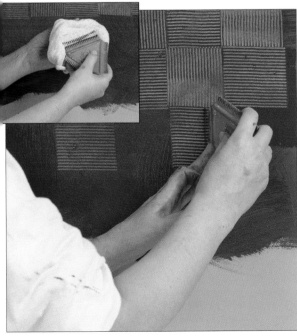

*3* *Wipe off excess glaze at frequent intervals. After a couple of rows you may find it easier and quicker to comb all the horizontal squares in a row, leaving gaps between them.*

*4* *Complete the pattern by combing vertical squares in the remaining gaps. Instead of squares you could also make diamond shapes by using the comb diagonally.*

## Alternatives

A vast range of effects can be produced by combing. The size of teeth, direction of the strokes, and color combinations can all be varied with interesting results.

RIGHT *A graduated comb was used first in one direction and then the opposite while the glaze was still wet.*

ABOVE *Green glaze was painted and combed over a red background. When dry, bright blue was combed across in the opposite direction.*

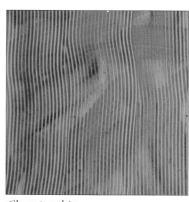

ABOVE *Different effects were obtained on this blue glaze over a white basecoat, using combs with different size teeth.*

LEFT *Brown glaze on off-white was combed in a random criss-cross way on the top part of the wall. Underneath, bright blue glaze on terra-cotta was combed leaving regular gaps.*

## PITFALLS

The right consistency of glaze is critical for achieving the characteristic sharp contrast and smooth lines of combing. If the glaze is too thick (near right), the lines will be blurred, indistinct, and form ridges; if it is too thin (far right), the effect will be thin and watery. To check the consistency of glaze practice on a small area first.

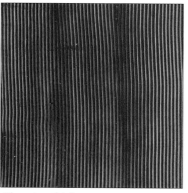

*Glaze too thick*

*Glaze too thin*

## Blue and Yellow Table

*TOP, ABOVE AND RIGHT This small
table was combed with several patterns to give a lively
effect. Yellow glaze was applied in selected areas over
blue paint and each leg was given a different treatment.
A large area on top was left unglazed to heighten
the impact of the combed pattern.*

## COLOR COMBINATIONS

*Dark brown on
bright green*

*Bright red on
dark blue*

*White on
bright blue*

*Light gray-green
on dark green*

### Chest of Drawers

*LEFT A small drawer unit was painted all over
in deep blue-black. White glaze was painted on
the drawers and combed with a homemade
comb the same width as the drawers. Alternate
drawers were combed again to make a strong
but irregular vertical stripe. On the remaining
drawers the first layer was left to dry, and a
second layer of white glaze was combed on
horizontally to make a checkered pattern.*

### Wooden Chest

*LEFT A simple wooden chest was painted
soft mauve, then combed over with a
graduated comb in a darker brown-purple.
The subtle effect suggests woodgraining.*

# Dragging & Flogging

D RAGGING AND FLOGGING ARE two techniques that derive from wood-graining. They replicate this effect when carried out in appropriate wood-toned colors. When used with more varied colors they are decorative techniques in their own right, traditionally used on both plaster walls and woodwork. Historically, dragging was used from the ceiling to the dado rail, with marbled or stippled panels below. There is a subtle difference between the two finishes: dragging produces smooth stripes, while the flogging breaks up the stripes and creates a more uniform overall effect.

**Kitchen Cupboard**
*Contrasting colors and techniques were used to decorate this simple kitchen cupboard. The top drawer front and door panels were painted light blue. Green glaze was dragged over this along the longest dimension. When dry, a second layer of the same green glaze was dragged at right angles to the first stripe. The remaining areas were painted middle-blue and darker blue glaze was dragged over it.*

## DRAGGING IN CLOSE-UP

Dragging uses a long, coarse-bristled brush and produces a pattern of broken stripes of different lengths. Brush widths range from 2½ to 12in/62½ to 300mm. Dragging on plaster walls is done vertically, but on wood it should follow the grain.

## TOOLS & MATERIALS

*Glaze brush*

*Dragging brush*

*Cloth for wiping off glaze*

*Mixed glaze*

# The Basic Technique: Dragging

*1 Paint on the glaze, spreading it out evenly. Paint vertically in strips to obtain uniform coverage.*

*2 Brush out the glaze as much as possible to create a thin glaze layer. The surface should not feel sticky.*

*3 Using the dragging brush, draw the brush up and down, holding it almost parallel to the surface. This will give an even, vertical stripe. The effect should be smooth and without ridges. Leave a wet edge to work into later.*

*4 To soften the effect hold the brush at almost 90 degrees to the surface and brush up and down at a slight angle to the stripes.*

*5 Continue on the next strip, working the glaze into the previous wet edge and repeat Steps 3–4 until you have covered the whole surface.*

# Dragging a Door

Treat the parts of the door in the order they are numbered above. Always drag in the same direction as the grain of the wood.

*1* Start applying the glaze in the top center stile (number 1 on the door). Stiles are vertical and rails horizontal.

*2* Thoroughly spread out the glaze as evenly as possible, for a smooth and uniform coverage.

*3* With a dragging brush, drag the glaze down over the whole top center stile and onto the rail.

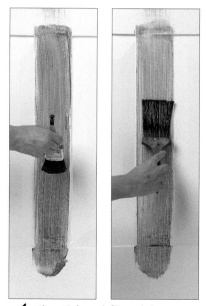

*4* Glaze (above left) and drag (above right) the bottom center stile (number 2 on the door).

**6** *Finally treat the two outer stiles (numbers 6 and 7), which extend the whole length of the door, making a neat join with the rails.*

**5** *Starting at the top of the door, paint the glaze horizontally on the rails (numbers 3, 4, and 5) then drag across. Take care to leave a neat edge against the already dragged stiles.*

# Dragging Below a Cornice

**1** *When applying the glaze, leave an unglazed gap at the top of the wall near the cornice so the glaze will not be too heavy at this spot. Spread out the glaze vertically with the dragging brush.*

**2** *Having wiped excess glaze off the brush on a paper towel (inset), hold the brush against the wall just below the cornice or rail, and apply a little pressure to the tip with the edge of your hand. This will release enough glaze to spread up to the top of the wall.*

# Dragging with a Cloth

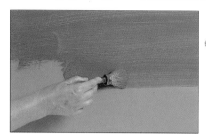

**1** *Paint a contrasting glaze on the surface where a base color has already been applied.*

**2** *Pull a bunched-up soft cloth across the surface in a straight line without stopping in the middle.*

**Cloth Dragged Table**
*ABOVE This alternative method of dragging gives a very soft effect. It may be difficult to keep the lines straight, but aligning them visually with an edge and always working in the same direction will help.*

## PITFALLS

When insufficient pressure is applied to the brush you will not achieve evenly striped dragging and the glaze will be patchy. If you bend your arm as you pull the brush down you will create a curved stroke. To avoid this, make shorter strokes so you can keep your arm straight. Mentally align the brush itself with a straight edge, rather than watching the mark left by it.

*Not enough pressure*

*Curved stripes*

# Dragging with a Flogging Brush

*A flogging brush is used in the same way as the dragging brush but produces a more pronounced striped effect. This can be particularly effective on furniture, and where the colors chosen are close in tone.*

## COLOR COMBINATIONS

*Dark green on bright green*

*Terra-cotta on bright pink*

*Off-white on varnished wood*

*Black on bright red*

### Chest of Drawers

*ABOVE A bright emerald base color had black glaze dragged over it. This toned down the brightness of the green and the contrast between the two colors has given a slightly antiqued look to this chest.*

### Tartan Effect

*ABOVE Terra-cotta and blue stripes were dragged over an egg-yolk yellow basecoat. The stripes are the same width as the brush.*

### Dragging a Wall

*LEFT A red terra-cotta glaze was dragged over a greenish-gray basecoat. Since the colors are close in tone, the result is even and subtle.*

FLOGGING IN CLOSE-UP

## FLOGGING IN CLOSE-UP

Flogging brushes have much longer bristles than dragging brushes. These produce a light stripe broken up by many small swirls. The final effect is linear, like dragging, but the stripes are broken up and more subtle. As with dragging, flogging on walls is done vertically but on wood it follows the grain.

## TOOLS & MATERIALS

*Flogging brush*

*Glaze brush*

*Mixed glaze*

# The Basic Technique: Flogging

*1* Apply the glaze, spreading it out thinly with the brush to form an even layer. As in dragging, paint in vertical strips to obtain uniform coverage.

*2* Direct the flogging brush up and down over the glaze to emphasize the striped effect. The surface should be a little wetter than when dragging. Leave an unflogged wet edge to join the next strip.

*3* Wipe off excess glaze from the brush. Starting at the bottom and using a sharp action, hit the surface with the top 2–3 in/ 50–75 mm of the brush, moving up about ¼ in/6.25 mm each time.

# Flogging with Feathers

A blue glaze was thinly painted over a yellow ocher background, and hit with a bunch of feathers, starting at the base and moving upward. This gives a more random result than using a brush. Use any feathers that are long, strong, and fairly flexible – pheasant and peacock feathers for example.

## COLOR COMBINATIONS

Black on dark pink

Gray on gray-blue

Pale yellow on blue-green

Terra-cotta on primrose yellow

## Flogged Stool

BELOW An olive green glaze was flogged with a brush over a pale cream basecoat to match the fabric of the seat.

## Decorative Shelf

ABOVE This gothic-inspired shelf with its integral decorative bracket was flogged, using a brush, in middle-brown over a dark cream basecoat. This gives a subtle suggestion of the grain of wood without trying to imitate wood too accurately.

# Patterning with Cloth

**Cloth Patterned Wall and Frame**

*The bright yellow wall and viridian green frame were covered with orange-terracotta glaze and dark blue-green glaze respectively, and then patterned with cheesecloth/mutton cloth to give it a lightly mottled look.*

THIS TECHNIQUE GIVES a cloudy, softly mottled finish. The fabric used is a fine-gauge, slightly elastic cotton knit. It is formed into a rounded pad by rolling the fabric and then tucking the ends inside the roll. The pad must be absolutely smooth since any folds in the fabric will make lines in the glaze. The delicate print of the weave is left on the glazed surface, creating a deliberately slightly uneven texture. To emphasize this, the pad can be dabbed more firmly in some areas than others. With careful application of glaze and even dabbing, the effect can be almost as regular as that made by stippling.

## TOOLS & MATERIALS

*Brush for applying glaze*

*Cheesecloth/ mutton cloth made into a pad*

*Mixed glaze*

# The Basic Technique

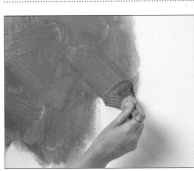

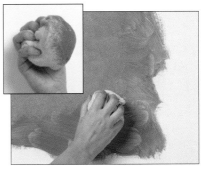

*1* Paint the glaze on generously. Use a strongly colored glaze to avoid patchiness, as the cheesecloth/mutton cloth will absorb the paint unevenly.

*2* Fold the cheesecloth/mutton cloth into a smooth pad. Dab it firmly over a small area. Move quickly on to the next area so the dabs overlap.

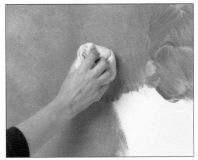

*3* Brush more glaze into the wet edge to prepare a new area for patterning. Spread out the paint evenly and brush well into the previous area.

*4* Continue dabbing carefully. When the pad is saturated with glaze, turn or refold it to a clean surface to avoid reapplying glaze to the surface.

# How to Tear a Cheesecloth/Mutton Cloth

*1* To avoid using scissors, which create small threads that stick to the work, pull the end of a thread running the width of the fabric.

*2* While holding the thread, push the gathered fabric along it until the thread either breaks or is pulled out.

*3* The cloth can now be pulled apart and there are no raw ends to ravel.

# Patterning a Corner with Cloth

**1** *Paint the glaze on both walls and into the corner. Avoid letting too much glaze accumulate in the angle.*

**2** *Fold the cloth to make a small edge that fits right into the corner without removing glaze from the other wall.*

# Creating a Mottled Effect

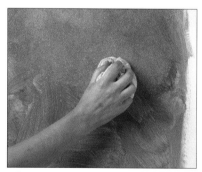

**1** *Brush on the glaze, covering the surface well using bold, uneven strokes.*

**2** *Having folded the cheesecloth/ mutton cloth into a smooth pad, dab it all over the surface.*

**3** *Refold the pad to a clean part, then dab patches of the surface again to remove more glaze from some areas than others.*

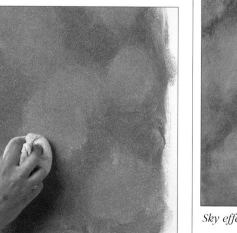

## ALTERNATIVES

You can use other types of cloth to create different effects depending on the weave.
A cloth with a coarser weave will produce a more textured look (below).

The sky effect (bottom) was produced by painting blue glaze unevenly over a white basecoat. After cloth patterning all over the surface, use a clean cloth to remove more glaze in patches, suggesting clouds.

*Using a coarse-weave cloth*

*Sky effect*

## COLOR COMBINATIONS

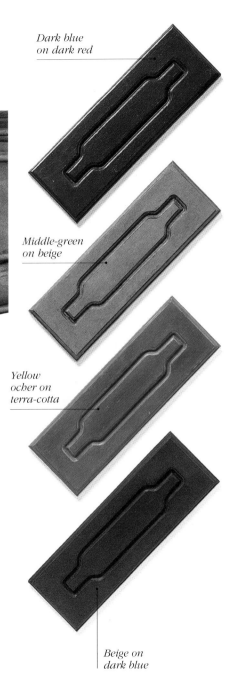

*Dark blue on dark red*

*Middle-green on beige*

*Yellow ocher on terra-cotta*

*Beige on dark blue*

## Cloth Patterned Fireplace

*ABOVE AND RIGHT Olive green glaze on a brown-gray basecoat was dabbed off with cheesecloth/ mutton cloth. A smaller piece of cloth was used to clean areas where too much glaze settled.*

## Cloth Patterned Frame

*LEFT The delicate finish on this frame picks up the colors in the picture. A deep mustard ocher glaze was applied over a dark green basecoat and evenly patterned.*

## PITFALLS

If the glaze is dabbed off unevenly the brushmarks will still show in some areas. Dabbing needs to be done systematically and evenly. If too little pressure is applied the same problem of visible brushstrokes will occur.

*Uneven dabbing*

# Rag Rolling

R AG ROLLING PRODUCES SUBTLE and complex-looking effects because it involves two paint techniques. First the surface is stippled (see pp. 38–43). The layer of glaze is hit firmly with a stippling brush, creating an even effect, then, while the glaze is still wet, a crumpled rag is rolled over it. This removes some of the glaze and reveals the base color. The delicacy of the stippling combined with the light, informal texture of the rag rolling is particularly elegant, especially when two soft, harmonizing colors of similar hue are chosen. More dramatic, contrasting combinations can be effective too. When rag rolling walls, it is quicker and easier for two people to work together. One person can apply and stipple the glaze over a floor to ceiling strip, while the other follows and does the rag rolling.

## RAG ROLLING IN CLOSE-UP

This close-up view clearly shows the characteristic texture achieved by rag rolling. The pattern created by rolling off the glaze with the cloth makes the painted surface resemble crumpled fabric.

## TOOLS & MATERIALS

*Glaze brush*

*Mixed glaze*

*Stippling brush*

*Cotton rag*

# The Basic Technique

*1 First apply the glaze evenly, spreading it out as much as possible. Then hit the surface firmly with the stippling brush (see p. 39), covering a small patch at a time and overlapping as you move on. Leave a wet edge to work into later.*

*2 Crumple a cotton cloth as for ordinary ragging (see p. 23). Do not form it into a smooth shape.*

*3 Holding the cloth firmly but not tightly, roll it upward. Leave an area of stippling to join with the next stippling band.*

*4 If gaps are left by the rolling process, you can dab over them with the cloth to make the pattern more even.*

# Rag Rolling a Corner

**1** Roll the crumpled rag up the wall as near to the corner as possible but without rubbing glaze off the other wall.

**2** Using a corner of the rag (or a smaller piece of cloth), dab right into the angle. Press lightly to avoid removing too much glaze.

## RAG ROLLING WITH CHAMOIS LEATHER

Chamois leather, a very soft and absorbent material, leaves a strong and distinct pattern. Used wet, it creates a more definite pattern. Used dry, a chamois gives a softer, more muted look. The results of both are shown below – attractively textured surfaces resembling crushed velvet.

*Using a dry chamois*

*Using a wet chamois*

### Storage Unit
*ABOVE Rag rolling can be used to create a lively, contemporary look. Onto five bright, sharp base colors – orange, red, yellow, green, and blue – a clear blue glaze was stippled then rag rolled. The glaze layer successfully unites the different base colors.*

### Wastepaper Basket
*LEFT The basket was painted a strong, deep red inside and out. Olive green glaze was stippled and rag rolled on the outside. The rich colors are particularly suited to the traditional style of the container.*

## Rag Rolled Wall

*RIGHT The wall was painted dark green, then a pale green glaze was rag rolled in stripes, leaving a narrow strip of dark green visible in between.*

## Hexagonal Box

*BELOW AND BELOW RIGHT The same yellow was used as the base color of both the box and its lid, uniting the two. Bright scarlet was then rag rolled on the lid and warm chocolate glazes on the box.*

## COLOR COMBINATIONS

*Middle-green on yellow ocher*

*Yellow ocher on dark red*

*Blue-green on pale green*

*Terra-cotta red on beige*

## PITFALLS

As you roll up the walls, the cloth may slip, wiping off a patch of glaze. Avoid this by working over a small area at a time. To correct it, apply a little glaze over the bare patch, stipple it, and dab off with a cloth.

The degree of contrast between glaze color and base color is critical in rag rolling. The dark green stippling (below) is too harsh against the white base; a softer, paler glaze color would have looked better.

*Smears*

*Tonal Contrast*

# Frottage

HIS PAINT EFFECT IS achieved without glaze. Instead you apply watered-down paint over a dry painted surface and lay paper or a similar absorbent material over the wet paint, flattening it out with your hands. Some of the paint is absorbed by the paper. When the paper is removed, a random pattern of paint is left. Each new sheet of paper and fresh layer of paint produces a different effect. Although the characteristic look of frottage is achieved primarily by chance, there are ways in which it can be controlled. The absorbency of the base paint, the choice of colors and the length of time the paper is left on are all factors influencing the end result.

**Frottaged Wall**

*Slate blue was frottaged over an olive brown basecoat. Frottage tends to produce an irregular effect, as here, with the base color showing through more clearly in some places than others.*

# The Basic Technique

Part of the unique texture produced by frottage is the small lines that are created by the "grain" of the newspaper.

## TOOLS & MATERIALS

*Brush for applying paint*

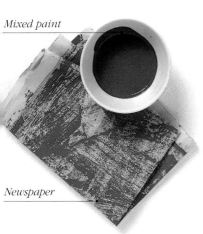

*Mixed paint*

*Newspaper*

*1* Mix the paint to the required consistency: it should be approximately two-thirds paint to one-third water. The mix may have to be adjusted according to the type of paint and the surface. Hold the newspaper up to the wall and mark the area it covers.

*2* Cover the marked out area with a fairly generous amount of paint. Work quickly before it dries out.

*3* Lay a sheet of newspaper over the wet painted surface. Smooth all over with the palm of your hands, taking care to apply even pressure so you will not leave hand prints.

*4* Peel off the paper carefully with one hand while still holding it in place with the other.

# *Joining Frottage Areas*

*1* Move on to the next area, applying the paint up to the edge of the finished area.

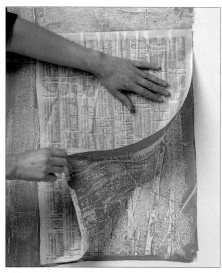

*2* Place the paper down on the newly painted surface and then remove it as in steps 3 and 4 of the Basic Technique.

*3* There are dark lines where each new frottaged area begins. To hide these, use double frottage (see opposite).

## PITFALLS

When there is a too strong a color contrast between the basecoat and the topcoat, the effect is somewhat coarse (below left): for a more subtle effect choose two colors closer in tone. It is also very important that the topcoat is of the right consistency. If you dilute it with too much water the paint will become very runny, resulting in visible drips in some areas (below center). If very little water is added the effect is very dense and heavy, losing the typical texture of frottage (below right).

*Colors too strong*

*Too much water added*

*Too little water added*

# Double Frottage

The reason why you might choose double frottage is to change the color effect and also either to emphasize or camouflage the shapes left by the paper. As you can see, this technique builds up a richly textured surface and offers endless opportunities for variations.

*1* *Coat a small part of your frottaged surface with diluted paint in a contrasting color. You can cover a larger area once you learn how quickly the paint dries.*

*2* *Tear off irregularly shaped and sized pieces of newspaper and lay them over the whole of the painted area while it is still wet.*

*3* *Smooth your hands all over the paper to ensure even contact with the paint.*

*4* *Peel off the paper. The finished effect shows how the regular rectangles and straight lines of the first paint layer have been hidden. Lines where one patch ends are inevitable to some extent, but can be minimized by using, as here, regularly shaped pieces of paper for the first layer and irregularly shaped pieces for the second layer only.*

## FROTTAGE WITH OTHER MATERIALS

Crumpled tissue paper gives a smaller, more even pattern than newspaper. Here (below), blue was frottaged over a red basecoat. Finely woven cotton was used to frottage the warm orange-brown and green, and blue stripes over the pale orange basecoat (right).

*Crumpled tissue paper*

*Cotton strip*

*Piece of cotton*

*Frottage with tissue paper*

*Frottage with fabric and three colors*

### Double Frottage

*ABOVE Reddish brown paint was frottaged over a grayish brown basecoat. To soften the effect yellow ocher was frottaged over this.*

### Hanging Box

*ABOVE The warm yellow ocher basecoat and rich terra-cotta topcoat complement each other well on this box. Pieces of paper were torn to the correct width in order to frottage inside the compartments.*

## COLOR COMBINATIONS

*Dark blue
on bright
red*

### Frottaged Desk

*LEFT AND BELOW* Rich
dark green was painted
and then frottaged over
a deep red basecoat.
The dark colors suit the
classic shape of the desk
and give a convincingly
antique effect, as shown
in the close-up.

*Off-white
on light
blue*

*Dark
green on
turquoise
blue*

### Frottaging a Chair

*LEFT AND ABOVE* The chair was
painted a strong, bright orange and
then frottaged over with a cooler blue
paint. The bold, strongly contrasting
colors give the chair a lively modern
look, showing how versatile this
technique can be.

*Dark red
on blue-
green*

# Woodgraining

**Woodgrained Chair**

*A simple, 1930s-style chair was given a maple-effect grain by using a warm, ginger-colored glaze over a yellow ocher basecoat. The baseboard was grained to match. The close-up detail shows how a darker glaze on the center panel gives a more pronounced grain.*

U SING PAINT TO IMITATE wood is a very old craft. It has probably been practiced for 200 years using the same techniques as today. Although wood can seem intimidating, it is not really a difficult technique. The wood effects shown here, mahogany, oak, and maple, exemplify a range of basic techniques and illustrate the use of essential tools. Once the basics are mastered, these skills can be adapted to reproduce numerous other woods. Achieving a convincing finish can seem quite daunting, but accurate color makes an enormous difference to the result and so careful study of real wood will pay off. Using the correct tools will also help, but you may prefer to try out some of the techniques with adapted tools and brushes before investing.

## TOOLS & MATERIALS

*Glaze*

*Flat brush for applying glaze and graining maple*

*Flogging brushes of different widths for oak and mahogany*

*Cork cut to wedge shape*

*Cotton rag to cover cork for oak graining*

*Fine cotton or open-weave cloth*

*Steel combs with different teeth sizes*

*Badger-hair softening brush*

*Mottler for mahogany*

# *Mahogany Graining*

Mahogany graining is best used on surfaces that are large enough to show the characteristic arch-shaped heart or "flame" to its best advantage. The sample below shows a warm, deep red mahogany, an effect which is recreated by painting dark chocolate brown glaze over a dark reddish-pink basecoat.

*1* Paint on the glaze vertically with a flat brush. Spread it out so the basecoat is visible (inset). Using a dry flogging brush, tap the bristles at 1 in/25 mm intervals, working up from the bottom.

*2* Dry off the flat brush. Create a half arch shape by moving the sides of the bristles in a wavy diagonal. Move up in successive arches, varying the pressure (but not too regularly) to resemble light and dark grain.

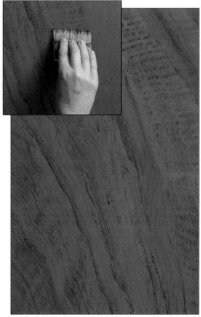

*3* To vary the shapes you make, twist the brush so that the bristles are at right-angles to the surface.

*4* Pull the mottler down in some areas, following the arch shape. Vary pressure to make darker and lighter marks, imitating mahogany's undulating grain.

# Oak Graining

To show off the beauty of oak graining you need a fairly large area, such as a door. The finish is easier to achieve on a flat or only slightly curved surface. Oak graining can look cool and delicate when you use creams and grays, or warm when rich or dark brown glazes are chosen. For the middle-brown color shown below, use burnt umber glaze over a cream basecoat.

*1* *Work in panels about 18in/45cm wide and 1 or 2 yards/1–2 meters high – like planks of real wood – according to the area being covered. Apply the glaze vertically with a flat brush.*

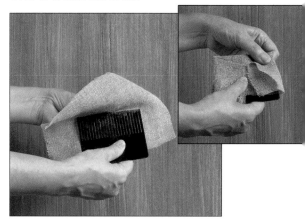

*2* *Fold a piece of fine cotton or open-weave cloth around a wide-toothed metal comb, tucking the edges in so that it is easy to handle.*

*3* *Pull the covered comb downward in a vertical line, twisting it very slightly to left and right to achieve the wavy look of real wood.*

*4* *While the glaze is still wet, go over the surface with a finer-toothed comb. Work at a slight diagonal to break up the vertical lines and make the light "dashes" typical of oak grain.*

# Graining with a Cork

**1** *You can imitate the small half-arch shapes that appear on oak by using a cork. Sharpen a cork to a wedge shape and wrap it in a cloth.*

**2** *Draw small half-arch shapes, making them look random by pressing harder at first, then relaxing the pressure. Group them together in areas and leave other patches free. Study real oak to see where these marks occur so you can reproduce them convincingly.*

# Maple Graining

This is a soft, delicate effect, particularly good on small items such as frames, boxes, and lamp bases. Below, a light, warm brown glaze is used over a honey-colored basecoat. For a richer look, a yellow ocher basecoat could be used, or a pink-toned basecoat with a chocolate brown glaze. This technique can be adapted to achieve a satinwood or rosewood effect.

**1** *Apply the glaze in one direction with a flat brush, spreading it out so the basecoat shows through.*

**2** *While the glaze is still wet, gently twist a mottler from side to side while moving it over the surface. Press on the bristles when changing direction to release more glaze, giving spots of color typical of maple.*

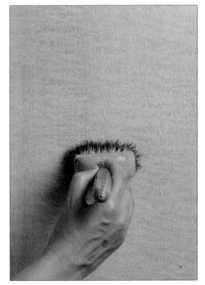

**3** *Before the glaze is dry brush over the surface with a softening brush to blend in the darker areas. Do not make the color too uniform. You can omit this stage if you like the effect already achieved.*

## Woodgraining Alternatives

*The details show oak graining (right) on pale gray, with darker gray glaze; bird's-eye maple (below) in rich, warm colors with minimum contrast between tones; and walnut graining (below right) in paler, colder colors, here, cool brown on greenish-yellow ocher.*

*Oak graining (above)*

*Maple graining (above)*

*Walnut graining (right)*

## Grained Tabletop

*RIGHT This elegant tabletop shows maple graining used to simulate different wood veneers. Different shades of brown glaze were used and it was softened on the paler areas to recreate the look of satinwood. The black banding and stenciled motif imitate ebony effectively.*

## Tall Shelf Unit

*ABOVE This unit is made from old, rough wood. Its rustic look was emphasized by the deliberately strong contrast between the reddish-pink basecoat and the brown glaze, which was deepened with a little dark blue.*

### Decorative Wooden Case

*BELOW The main panel was grained to imitate burr walnut with dark brown glaze over an orange basecoat. The central motif was stenciled on and glaze was dabbed on and blended, using a softening brush, to resemble satinwood. The outer band was initially treated using the mahogany technique and adapted to imitate rosewood.*

### Coal Bucket

*ABOVE This old metal coal bucket has a new lease of life as a decorative object with an oak grain treatment, a typical Victorian effect. At that time metal was beginning to replace wood for many domestic items, but since it was an unfamiliar material it was often disguised to look like wood.*

## PITFALLS

Important tips for achieving convincing wood finishes are to judge the colors carefully and to mix a translucent glaze that will not mask the base color. In the example (below left) too little glaze has been used over the basecoat, so the effect is dull and opaque. The detail (below center) shows the crude result when the glaze color and basecoat contrast too sharply. The example (below right) shows how unrealistic graining looks when the brushmarks are painted too evenly.

*Not enough glaze*

*Wrong colored basecoat*

*Brush marks too regular*

# Decorative Graining

**Decoratively Grained Wall**

*This boldly colored modern room uses almost complementary shades of scarlet and blue to dramatic effect. Gray-blue glaze was grained with the "oak" edge of the roller (see p. 80).*

**W**ITH WOODGRAINING the intention is to imitate natural wood as closely as possible. However, you can also achieve a colorful and decorative effect with different types of flexible combs and rollers. The purpose is not to create a totally convincing replica, but to produce the look of painted oak and pine quickly and easily. The same method can be used to simulate moiré silk or other fabrics. You can experiment with overlaying patterns and colors, remembering that this technique is more suited to bold than subtle effects.

## TOOLS & MATERIALS

*Plastic graining roller with removable head for wide or thin grains*

*Soft plastic graining combs with two different widths*

*Glaze*

*Cloth to wipe off excess glaze from comb and surface*

*Flogging brush for softening*

*Brush for applying glaze*

# The Basic Technique

**1** *Apply the glaze vertically, brush it out to give a thin translucent covering. Wipe over with a soft cloth so that only a very thin layer of glaze is left.*

**2** *Apply the top of the roller to the glazed surface. Rock the roller halfway down its length to achieve the grained effect, the top of the head gives the broad effect of oak grain.*

**3** *Work down the wall from the top, rocking the roller very slightly at intervals. You may want to use both hands to ensure firm contact with the surface.*

**4** *Remove excess glaze built up at the top of the head with a soft cloth (inset). You can achieve the narrower effect of pine grain by rocking the roller all the way down and then up again. This produces characteristic circular knot shapes. Space these irregularly.*

# Softening the Pattern

The grained effect can be left as previously shown, but if you want to heighten the look of moiré silk rather than wood, or simply to make the effect less strong, the finish can be softened with a flogging, dragging, or softening brush. A flogging brush, as used below, emphasizes the fabric effect. This is enhanced even more if a soft color similar to the glaze is used for the base.

*Using the flogging brush, lightly pull down the bristles over the thin and still slightly wet glaze. This will blur the edges of the "knots".*

*To accentuate the look of fabric and soften the effect even more, the flogging brush can be brushed across horizontally as well as vertically.*

# Different Types of Grain

*These pictures (right) show the different surfaces of the graining roller heads and the oak and pine effects they can create.*

*Oak effect*

*Pine effect*

## COLOR COMBINATIONS

### Bedside Cabinet
*LEFT This small cabinet was painted dark blue and a grayish white glaze was applied over it. The graining comb was used just to make a swirling pattern rather than to imitate wood.*

### Picture Frame
*ABOVE Green glaze was painted over a reddish-brown basecoat. Since the comb was wider than the frame, only the middle section of the roller was used. The result is a woodgrained look, but in deliberately unnatural colors.*

*Brown on beige*

*Light blue on dark blue*

*Strong green on clear yellow*

*Strong pink on bright pink*

## PITFALLS

If the glaze is too thick and wet, the graining looks heavy. Here, the color also contrasts too strongly with the white background and the graining is too regular for it to have a natural look. Avoid repeating the rocking motion too often, since it creates unattractive breaks and lines across the grain.

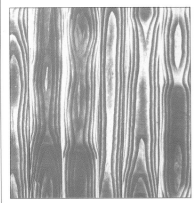

*Too heavily lined*

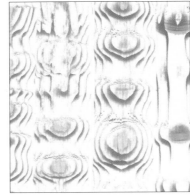

*Broken grain*

# Marbling

## Marbled Chest

*The panels of this chest were marbled using a soft, warm raw sienna deepened with a little raw umber. After the initial layer of glaze was applied, the panels were sponged, ragged, and veined. The surrounds were painted a deep green-blue.*

**M**ARBLING, LIKE WOODGRAINING, is a technique in which one material is painted to imitate another. To achieve a convincing result it is important to study examples of real marble. But because real marble comes in so many different colors and patterns, you can work more freely than when woodgraining. Marbling techniques are very flexible. The first step is the subtle blending of softened tones but then other methods, such as sponging, splattering, or veining with artist's brushes or a feather, can be used separately or together. Marbling is traditionally done on structural surfaces, such as walls, floors, and pillars but it can be just as effective on small items, such as lamp bases, boxes, and frames. The finished work should be sealed with gloss or semigloss varnish (see pp. 18–19) both to protect the surface and give it the shiny look of real marble.

## TOOLS & MATERIALS

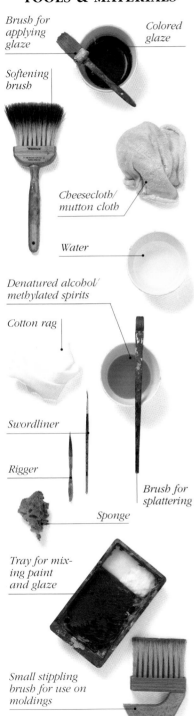

Brush for
applying
glaze

Colored
glaze

Softening
brush

Cheesecloth/
mutton cloth

Water

Denatured alcohol/
methylated spirits

Cotton rag

Swordliner

Rigger

Sponge

Brush for
splattering

Tray for mix-
ing paint
and glaze

Small stippling
brush for use on
moldings

# *The Basic Technique*

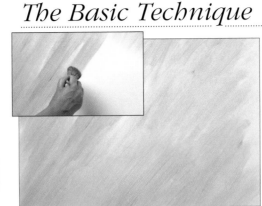

*1* Color the glaze, ensuring that it remains
transparent. Mix only a little at a time, this
way the shade of each batch will vary. Apply
the glaze diagonally, varying the angle and
thickness of the brushstrokes.

*2* Add darker paint to
the glaze and apply it
in patches, strengthening
some of the existing darker
areas. Aim to establish
three tones: light, medium,
and dark.

*3* Fold cheesecloth/mutton cloth
into a smooth pad and dab the
glaze in the lighter areas to remove
brushstrokes and even out the colors.

*4* Now dab the darker areas.
Treating dark and light areas
separately keeps them well defined
and contrasting.

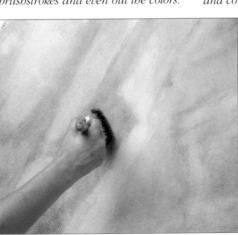

*5* While the glaze is still wet,
use the softening brush to
remove the cheesecloth/
mutton cloth marks. If you let
the glaze dry out you will be
unable to remove them. Hold
the brush at right angles to
the surface and move it from
side to side, using your arm,
not your wrist, to achieve a
smooth effect without creating
visible brushstrokes. You can
then add veins, if desired
(see pp. 84–85).

# Veining

It is not essential to add veins to make marbling look realistic, but although tricky to do well, veining can look very effective. Always work around the shapes and colors of the basic marbling, emphasizing and outlining the darker shapes. Veining is done with slightly thinned paint, not glaze, and in a color just a little darker than the base shade. Various tools can be used for veining, including artist's brushes, feathers, and a special brush used just for painting lines called a swordliner. You can use a rigger, a short smaller brush that makes thinner lines, to reduce veins that are too thick.

# Using Artist's Brushes

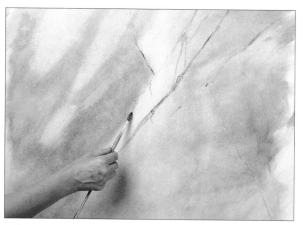

*1 Use a small artist's fitch, made of soft bristle, to outline darker areas or create veins of varying thickness. Do not hold the brush like a pencil, but allow it to move loosely so that the veins do not look too tightly drawn.*

*2 Go over the veins with a softening brush so that they gently blend into the background. Use the brush as in step 5 of* The Basic Technique *(see p. 83)*

*3 Lighten thick areas by dipping a rigger in water and removing a little paint to reveal the white base and form a lighter "island" within a vein (left). This can only be done while the paint is still wet. To soften the effect further, rag the veins gently with a cotton cloth to break up the veining slightly (above).*

# Using a Swordliner

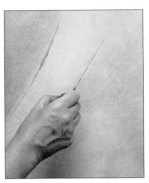

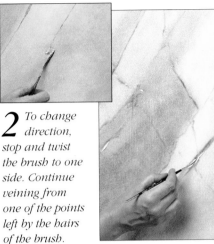

*1* *Use the tip of the brush to start the vein, then increase the pressure to broaden the line.*

*2* *To change direction, stop and twist the brush to one side. Continue veining from one of the points left by the hairs of the brush.*

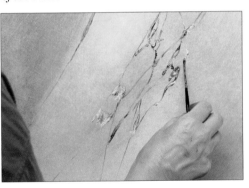

*3* *You can add to the veining with a rigger, complementing the shapes made by the swordliner. It is used in the same way – by stopping the line and twisting the brush.*

# Using a Feather

*Any long, strong feathers – such as goose, duck, or peacock – are suitable for veining. Use a feather with the longer barbs on the right for veins starting at the top left, and vice versa. Dip the feather in the paint, dab it on to the surface, then drag across it. Since the feather is curved, this may feel awkward at first, but this method produces authentically irregular veins.*

**PITFALLS**
If you drag the side rather than the tip of the softening brush along the surface you will get scratches (below).

Veining can look crude and artificial for several reasons. Here (bottom), the lines are too dark and positioned arbitrarily, without relating to the dark and light areas in the basecoat. The three lines at the top right are too evenly spaced and the wiggly line looks unnatural. The thickness of the lines is too regular. Veins should start at the side of the work and vary from thick to thin, eventually petering out altogether. Take care not to cross lines, as shown. The meeting point of veins should either form a little "island" or the line should continue on the other side a small distance away from the meeting point.

*Scratches*

*Artificial looking lines*

# Splatter Marbling

Some natural marbles have a pattern of small spots and few or no veins. Marbling to achieve this kind of effect is useful for small objects where an intense overall look is required. Splatter marbling is a technique that can be used on both horizontal and vertical surfaces and it can be used to cover a whole area or just part of a larger marbled surface to give a bit of variety.

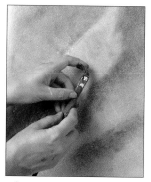

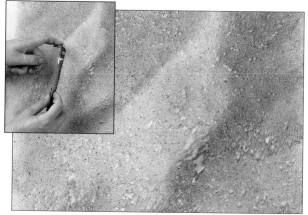

*1* While the basecoat is still wet, take a small stiff brush, dip it in water, and using your finger, splatter the water over the surface.

*2* Go over the area immediately with a softening brush to reveal the spots made by the water. Do this lightly or the spots will be smoothed out.

*3* For greater depth and variety mix a little darker paint with the water and splatter small areas. Soften gently. The final result is a mixture of light and dark spots of varying sizes.

# Marbling a Cornice

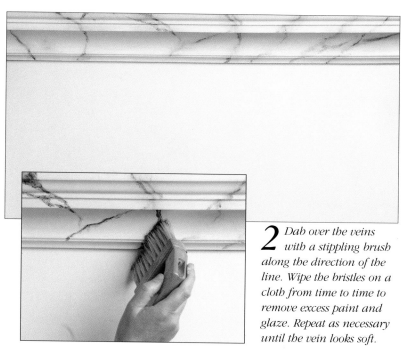

*1* Apply thin, clear, or light-colored glaze to the surface, taking care not to let glaze build up in the crevices. Paint on veins in a diagonal direction, varying the thickness of the lines. Apply the paint quite thinly so that the veins do not look heavy.

*2* Dab over the veins with a stippling brush along the direction of the line. Wipe the bristles on a cloth from time to time to remove excess paint and glaze. Repeat as necessary until the vein looks soft.

# Marbling Panels

 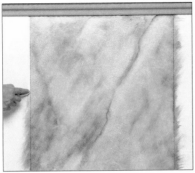 

*1* Real marble comes in slabs. For an authentic look on a wall divide it into suitably sized panels, marking the edges with a soft pencil.

*2* Marble a panel, then wipe off any glaze that has spread over the pencil line into the next panel.

*3* Marble every other panel and allow it to dry completely, preferably overnight. Then marble the unpainted panels in the same way.

*4* Wipe off any glaze that has gone onto the adjacent panel. The pencil line should show through and resemble the gap between slabs. It can be deepened with a darker pencil if desired.

*5* To harmonize the panels, you can add in some more veins at this stage, or veins can be darkened, as shown here, to match veining elsewhere.

# Floating Marble

Floating marble is a quick and effective technique that you can use on horizontal surfaces, such as tabletops and floors. Here, strong, bright colors are used, but the technique also works particularly well with very dark, more subtle shades such as the greens used on the plaque opposite. You can also do this technique using one color only to give an overall textured effect.

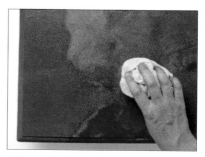

*1 Apply one colored glaze in patches, spreading it out well over the surface.*

*2 Paint the second color on the bare areas. With a smooth pad of folded cheesecloth/mutton cloth dab over first one color, then the other, using a clean part of the pad to avoid mixing and muddying the colors.*

*3 Go over the whole surface gently with a softening brush to even out the glaze.*

*4 Dip the softening brush in water and dab it all over the surface, forming small spots.*

*5 Next dip the softening brush in denatured alcohol/methylated spirits and dab it over the surface. The combination of glaze, water, and denatured alcohol/methylated spirits will produce spots and blotches of different sizes. Allow the surface to dry without softening it.*

## Picture Frame

*LEFT The floating technique was used here, with water, denatured alcohol/methylated spirits, and paint used alternately to build up layers of spots and patches. The off-white veins were painted on diagonally as if the whole frame were one piece of marble.*

## Floating Marbling on a Panel

*RIGHT Over a white basecoat, blue and terra-cotta glazes created this floating marble surface. This can be used on floors or any other flat surface.*

## Marbled Plaque

*RIGHT AND BELOW This plaster plaque was painted black and then glazed with several shades of dark green, using the floating method to reveal the layers and create spots of different colors.*

# Sponge Marbling

This technique is particularly suitable for small areas and objects. A sponge is dipped in water and then dabbed over the surface to lift off glaze, leaving lighter spots and blobs. Then darker paint is dabbed on for contrast. Experiment with doing more or less of the two stages to achieve a result you like.

Choose a sponge with large holes so the paint leaves a more positive mark.

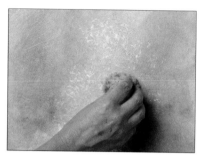

*2 Thin paint in a slightly darker shade than the glaze color so that it flows freely. Dip a clean sponge in the paint, using a tray so that the sponge can be squeezed out slightly so it is not too saturated. Dab the sponge on the darker areas, lightly at first to judge the effect. More layers can be built up for a more strongly contrasting look.*

*1 Apply the glaze so that there are dark and light areas. While the surface is still wet, dab over the lighter areas with a damp sponge.*

**Candlestick**

RIGHT *The effect here is of granite, achieved by the sponge method with first gray, then black glaze applied over an off-white basecoat.*

**Marbled Case**

ABOVE AND RIGHT *The border was painted to imitate dramatic black and sienna Porto d'Oro marble. The inner panel has a white basecoat painted over with very faint black veins to resemble Carrara marble, then stippled over slightly for a trompe-l'œil look.*

### Marbled Door

*LEFT Over a white basecoat, raw sienna, raw umber, and white were sponge marbled around the edge of this door, and splatter marbled on the inside panel. The effect is light and warm.*

### COLOR COMBINATIONS

Deep blue-green with white veins on gray

Beige with dark cool brown veins on white

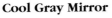

### Cool Gray Mirror

*ABOVE This mirror was painted white and splatter marbled with different proportions of ultra-marine blue, raw umber and white, giving a gray-blue looking, cold marble effect.*

Black veins on transparent glaze

### Splatter Marbled Candlestick

*LEFT A wooden candlestick was painted light, cool brown. The splatter technique was then applied using various proportions of raw umber and white. When this coat was dry a second layer using burnt sienna was randomly applied in the same way. The two layers of dark colors give the candlestick a solid, heavy look.*

White and terra-cotta on black

# Combining Techniques

USING DIFFERENT PAINT EFFECTS in combination with one another gives greater emphasis to the different part of the surface. You could marble, stipple, or comb a chair rail or dado rail, and then use a different technique, such as ragging, colorwashing, or patterning with cloth, on the wall above it. In the same way, you can highlight the different parts of a piece of furniture, with one effect on panels or tabletops and another for the panel surrounds or table legs.

Don't combine too many different techniques or they will detract from one another. Two techniques is normal, but on walls and larger furniture, three techniques can be used.

**Wall and Dado-rail**
*Off-white was covered with blue-gray for the colorwashed top and dragged dado, and terra-cotta for the combed area.*

*Colorwashing
(pp. 30–37)*

*Dragging
(pp. 50–55)*

*Combing
(pp. 44–49)*

Combing
(pp. 44–49)

Sponging
(pp. 26–29)

## Combed and Sponged Chest of Drawers

*Olive-green was combed over a red basecoat on the top and drawer fronts of this chest of drawers. The tree shapes were made by sponging on dark green, middle-green, and a little yellow-ocher.*

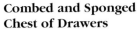

## Marbled and Dragged Candlestick

*The off-white basecoat was covered with white glaze and then marbled using a variety of blacks and ochers. A charcoal gray was dragged around the base.*

## Frottaged and Sponged Cupboard

*On the center panels, deep cherry pink was frottaged over the pale gray basecoat, while on the surrounds three colors – dark red, dark blue, and dark green were sponged on.*

Frottage
(pp. 66–71)

Sponging
(pp. 26–29)

Marbling
(pp. 82–91)

Dragging
(pp. 50–55)

# Index

# How to Find Supplies

The tools and materials you need for the techniques demonstrated in this book are generally available from speciality art supply and paint stores. To find a store near you, try looking in your local telephone directory under paint, art, craft supplies, or decorative materials. If you are on the Internet, you can look there under the same categories, or you can try speciality magazines on crafts and interior decoration, where many of the stores and suppliers place advertisements. If there are no stores in your neighborhood, don't despair as many of them have mail order facilities and you can send for a catalogue.

You can also visit Annie Sloan's Internet site – *www.anniesloan.co.uk* - for more information.

# Acknowledgments

This book could not have been produced without the tremendous assistance of the Home Team – David, Henry, Felix, and Hugo – and the Away Team – the photographer, Geoff Dann, his assistant, Gavin Durrant, and the designer, Steve Wooster. Many thanks also to Colin Ziegler, Claire Waite, and Gabrielle Townsend for their patience and understanding.

I am also very grateful to Eri Hz. Heiliggers who gave expert advice on woodgraining and provided the grained samples on page 76, the grained case on page 77, and the marbled case on page 90; and to Kate Pollard who assisted with the sponged table on page 26 and the colorwashed fireplace on page 30.

I used my own range of paints, pigments, and glazing medium throughout the book, but I would like to thank the following for providing other materials: Polyvine for the varnishes (Polyvine Ltd. Vine House, Rockhampton, Berkeley, Glos. GL13 9DT); R G Willis for the fire surround (Wessex Products Ltd. Unit 16 Harris Road, Calne Business Centre, Calne, Wilts. SN11 9PT); Finesse of Oxford for the plasterwork plaques, cornices, fireplace, and brackets (Finesse Ltd. Unit 5, 7 Westway, Botley, Oxford); and Sue Teichmann for the wastepaper basket.

Thanks also to Lewis Ward of Whistler Brushes, whose speciality brushes feature often throughout the book (Lewis Ward and Co., 128 Fortune Green Road, London, NW6) and all those at Relics of Witney, especially Bret Wiles, Chris Walker, and Ray Russell.